The Gracious Mother Goose

by Becky White

Illustrated by Warner McGee

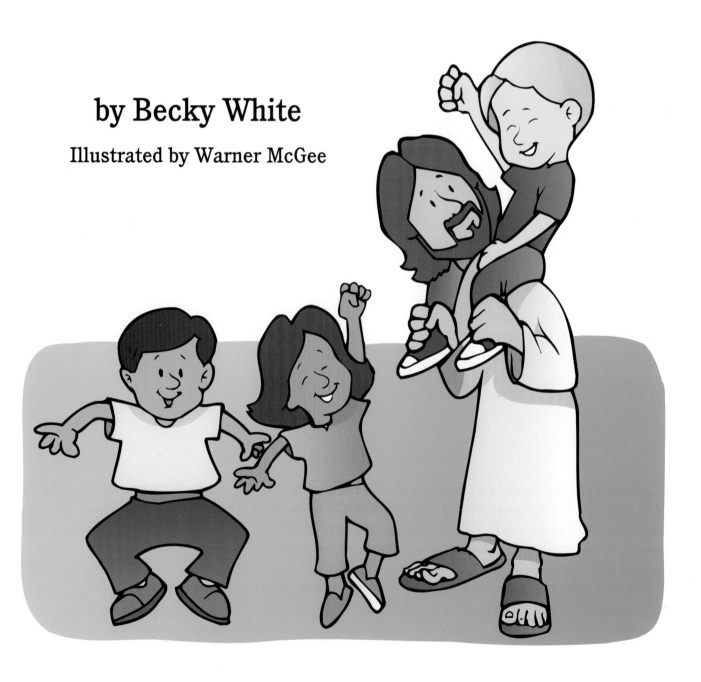

Carson-Dellosa Christian Publishing • Greensboro, North Carolina

For David
who gives my life
rhyme,
rhythm,
and reason.

Credits
Author: Becky White
Illustrator: Warner McGee
Editor: Carol Layton
Creative Director: Annette Hollister-Papp
Layout Design: Mark Conrad
Cover Design: Peggy Jackson

It is the mission of Carson-Dellosa Christian Publishing to create the highest–quality Scripture-based children's products that teach the Word of God, share His love and goodness, assist in faith development, and glorify His Son, Jesus Christ.

". . . teach me your ways so I may know you. . . ."
Exodus 33:13

Printed in the USA • All rights reserved.

ISBN 0-88724-217-0

Contents

Chapter 1 — Poems and Prayers

Poems

Prayers

Chapter 2— Mother Goose Goes Gospel

Chapter 3 — Jump Rope Rhymes, Riddles, and Nursery Games

Jump Rope Rhymes

Riddles

Nursery Games

Chapter 4 — Song and Dance

Chapter 5 — Bible Stories in Rhyme

Chapter 6 — Holiday Performances

Who Was Mother Goose?

According to one legend, Mother Goose was a Boston woman named Elizabeth, born in 1665. At age 27, she married Isaac Goose and became stepmother to his ten children. The couple went on to have six more children. It's not difficult to believe that Mrs. Goose could have written the lines: *There once was an old woman, who lived in a shoe. She had so many children, she didn't know what to do.* To her credit, there was a volume of rhymes allegedly published in 1719 by one of her sons-in-law titled, *Mother Goose's Melodies for Children.* Even though Elizabeth Goose was a real person, no copy of that book has ever been found.

Others believe that Mother Goose was actually a man named Charles Perrault. A book published in 1697 by Perrault was subtitled "Tales of My Mother Goose." But whether Mother Goose was the mother of sixteen, a man, or even someone else entirely, one thing is certain—Mother Goose rhymes are often the first verses that some children hear. Although some Mother Goose rhymes are proverbs or prayers, many others originated as tavern limericks, spoofs, satire, and lyrics of romantic songs. Some of the ancient rhymes are violent or bizarre. Yet for hundreds of years, these words have been put into impressionable young minds.

The Gracious Mother Goose brims with verses that teach Bible stories and eternal truths. Each page is captioned with Scripture to bring the pure Light of God's Word to children.

Chapter One
Poems and Prayers

These familiar rhymes have been transformed into Christ-honoring poems or prayers.
Read them to bless children with truths from God's Word and to give Jesus first place in everything!

And He is before all things, and in Him all things consist. And He is the head of the body, the church,
who is the beginning, the firstborn from the dead, that in all things He may have the preeminence.
Colossians 1:17-18 NKJV

Poems

Wee Willie Winkie

Wee Willie Winkie
Runs through the town,
Upstairs and downstairs,
Spreading news around.

Rapping at the window,
Crying at the lock,
"Do you know Jesus loves you,
And wants you in His flock?"

How beautiful on the mountains are the feet of those who bring good news. . . . Isaiah 52:7

Deedle, Deedle, Dumpling, My Son John

Deedle, deedle, dumpling, my son John,
Went to bed with his prayers all done.
One for father, one for mom,
Deedle, deedle, dumpling, my son John.

The prayer of a godly person is powerful. It makes things happen. James 5:16 NIrV

Polly and Sukey

Polly get your Bible out,
Polly get your Bible out,
Polly get your Bible out,
And let's read Psalms.

Sukey read some more to me,
Sukey read some more to me,
Sukey read some more to me,
I love every verse.

Oh, how I love your law! I meditate on it all day long. Psalm 119:97

Mary, Mary, Extraordinary!

Mary, Mary, extraordinary!
How does your faith in God grow?
By hearing the Word—the Word of the Lord,
And obeying it wherever I go.

So then faith comes by hearing, and hearing by the word of God. Romans 10:17 NKJV

Jack and Jill

Jack and Jill, of their own free will,
Waded into the water.
Despite their size,
They were both baptized.
God bless you, son and daughter.

*Anyone who believes
and is baptized
will be saved.*
Mark 16:16 NIrV

*Obey [your leaders] so
that their work will be
a joy. If you make
their work a heavy
load, it won't do
you any good.*
Hebrews 13:17 NIrV

Little Miss Lou

Little Miss Lou
Sat in a pew,
Popping her gum as she chewed.
Along came an usher
Who politely hushed her,
And taught her that love is not rude.

Old Woman Who Lived In a Shoe

There was an old woman, who lived in a shoe,
She had so many children, and loved them all, too!
She gave them broth and jam on bread,
Then sang them a lullaby, and sent them to bed.

*He gives children to the
woman who has
none. He makes
her a happy
mother. Praise
the Lord!*
Psalm 113:9 ICB

Come, My Dear Children

Come, my dear children,
Up is the sun,
Birds are all singing,
And morn has begun.

Up from the bed,
Greet a new day.
Your friends are waiting
For you to come play.

There's a Neat Little Clock

There's a neat little clock,
In the church hall it stands,
And it points to the time
With its two little hands.

And may we, like the clock,
Keep a face clean and bright,
With hands ever ready
To do what is right.

Little Boy Blue

Little Boy Blue,
Climb out of bed,
The church bell's calling,
"Wake up, Sleepyhead."

There is a time for everything, and a season for every activity under heaven. . . . Ecclesiastes 3:1

Hey Diddle Diddle

Hey diddle diddle,
Curt played the fiddle,
The crowd clapped their hands with the tune.
The little kids laughed
And begged for more,
But the music was over too soon.

*. . . a time to
weep and a time to
laugh. . . .*
Ecclesiastes 3:4a

*. . . a time to mourn and
a time to dance. . . .* Ecclesiastes 3:4b

Jack Spratt

Jack Spratt could play the fiddle,
His wife could sing and dance,
And so, between the two of them,
They nurtured their romance.

Goosey, Goosey, Gander

Goosey, goosey, gander, where do you wander?
Upstairs, and downstairs, and in my pastor's chamber.
There I saw an old man, his eyes closed in prayers.
I saw him kneeling, head bowed, so I crept down the stairs.

*. . . a time to be silent
and a time to speak. . . .*
Ecclesiastes 3:7b

——— **11** ——— CD-2038 *The Gracious Mother Goose*

Starlight, Star Bright

Starlight, star bright,
First star I've seen tonight,
Pray I may,
Pray I might,
Grow wiser
And have insight.

Starlight, star bright,
First star I've seen tonight.
Pray I may,
Pray I might,
Be peaceful
And slow to fight.

Starlight, star bright,
First star I've seen tonight.
Pray I may,
Pray I might,
Be gracious
Not impolite.

Starlight, star bright,
First star I've seen tonight.
Pray I may,
Pray I might,
Be loving
And do what's right.

Starlight, star bright,
First star I've seen tonight.
Pray I may,
Pray I might,
Be pleasing
In the Lord's sight.

May the words of my mouth and the meditation of my heart
be pleasing in your sight, O LORD, my Rock and my Redeemer.
Psalm 19:14

Adam Named the Animals

A Was an Archer

A was an alligator, sleeping in the bog.

B was a birdie, hiding on a log.

C was a caterpillar, covered with fuzz,

D was a donkey, just doin' what it does.

E was an elephant, trunk on its face.

F was a froggy, hopping in a race.

G was a gorilla, what a racket it could make.

H was a hippo, swimming in the lake.

I was for insects, that fly through the air,

J was for jaguar, asleep in its lair.

K was a kangaroo, hopping in the sand,

L was a lion, mighty and grand.

M was a mouse, nibbling on its cheese,

N was a nanny goat, gentle as you please.

O was an ostrich chick, fluffy with down,

P was a porcupine, in a needle gown.

Q was a queen bee, ruler of her hive.

R was a robin, that loves to swoop and dive.

S was a swan, a bird of charm and grace,

T was a toucan, a huge beak for a face.

U was a unicorn, a make-believe beast.

V was a vulture, looking for a feast.

W was a walrus, with tusks tough as nails,

X was an x-ray fish, with see-through scales.

Y was a yak, that you milk like a cow.

Z was a zebra, that won't pull a plow.

*He brought them to the man to see what he would name them;
and whatever the man called each living creature, that was its name.* Genesis 2:19

Prayers

God Bless the Father

God bless the father of this house,
The mother bless also,
And all the little children
That round the table go.

Little Fred Went to Bed

When little Fred went to bed,
He always said his prayers.
He kissed mamma, and then papa,
And hurried up the stairs.

Bless My Porridge

Bless my porridge hot,
Bless my porridge cold,
Bless all food inside my pot
In my loving household.

When you pray, be faithful. Romans 12:12 NIrV

Dickory, Dickory, Dock

Dickory, dickory, dock,
I pray around the clock.
I pray at dawn,
I pray at dusk,
Dickory, dickory, dock.

One, Two, Three

One, two, three,
I love Jesus
And Jesus loves me.
How good is He!
One, two, three,
I love Jesus
And Jesus loves me.

How great is the love the Father has given us so freely! 1 John 3:1 NIrV

Little Jack Horner

Little Jack Horner
Sat in a corner,
Eating a Christmas pie.
He bowed his head,
And closed his eyes,
And said, "No one's more blessed than I."

Spend a lot of time in prayer. Always be watchful and thankful. Colossians 4:2 NIrV

Chapter Two
Mother Goose Goes Gospel

These familiar rhymes have been adapted to teach Bible stories and truths.
Bless children by sharing the goodness of God and His Word!

An Old Widowed Mother

Old Mother Hubbard

An old widowed mother
Went to the cupboard
To get some food to boil.
But when she came there
The cupboard was bare,
Except for a pot of oil.

She said to Elisha,
"We've nothing to eat.
No wheat to bake bread,
No cheese, and no meat!

"I owe much money
That I can't repay.
And the lender is coming
To take my sons away!"

"Borrow pots from your neighbors,
Get all you can find.
Then bring them inside
And have peace of mind."

The widow obeyed him,
Then she closed the door.
She poured and she poured,
And poured some more.

"It's a miracle," she cried.
"Trust the Lord," he said.
Sell some for your debts,
With the rest, buy bread.

Read how the prophet Elisha multiplied a widow's oil in 2 Kings 4:1-7.

The World That God Made

The House That Jack Built

This is the world that God made.
This the sea, the sparkling sea
That wraps the world that God made.

This is the land, that divides the sea,
That wraps the world that God made.

This is the air, warmed by the sun,
That's above the land, that divides the sea,
That wraps the world that God made.

This is the rain, refreshing and clean,
That cools the air, warmed by the sun,
That's above the land, that divides the sea,
That wraps the world that God made.

This is the grass, knee-deep and green,
That's fed by the rain, refreshing and clean,
That cools the air, warmed by the sun,
That's above the land, that divides the sea,
That wraps the world that God made.

This is the cow that gives milk and cream,
That eats the grass, knee-deep and green,
That's fed by the rain, refreshing and clean,
That cools the air, warmed by the sun,
That's above the land, that divides the sea,
That wraps the world that God made.

This is the farmer, hardy and lean,
That milks the cow that gives milk and cream,
That eats the grass, knee-deep and green,
That's fed by the rain, refreshing and clean,
That cools the air, warmed by the sun,
That's above the land, that divides the sea,
That wraps the world that God made.

This is the woman, with a baby to wean,
That is wed to the farmer, hardy and lean,
That milks the cow that gives milk and cream,
That eats the grass, knee-deep and green,
That's fed by the rain, refreshing and clean,
That cools the air, warmed by the sun,
That's above the land, that divides the sea,
That wraps the world that God made.

This is the church, where bells dong and ding,
That summon the woman, with a baby to wean,
That is wed to the farmer, hardy and lean,
That milks the cow that gives milk and cream,
That eats the grass, knee-deep and green,
That's fed by the rain, refreshing and clean,
That cools the air, warmed by the sun,
That's above the land, that divides the sea,
That wraps the world that God made.

Through him all things were made; without him nothing was made that has been made.
In him was life, and that life was the light of men. John 1:3

I Love You Well, My Little Brother

I Love You Well, My Little Brother

I love you well, my little brother,
And you are fond of me.
Let us be kind to one another,
As brothers ought to be.
You shall learn to pray with me,
And learn to share my joys,
And then I think that we shall be
Two blessed little boys.

I love you well, my little sister,
And you are fond of me.
Let us be kind to one another,
As sisters ought to be.
You shall learn to comb my hair,
And I will brush your curls,
And then I think that we shall be
Two blessed little girls.

I love you well, my own dear mother,
And you are fond of me.
Let us be kind to one another,
As family ought to be.
You shall raise me till I'm grown,
And I will give you love,
And then I think that we shall be
Blessed by God above.

I love you well, my own dear father,
And you are fond of me.
Let us be kind to one another,
As family ought to be.
You will keep me safe and sound,
And I will honor you,
And then I think that we shall be
Well blessed by God, too.

How good and pleasant it is when brothers live together in unity! Psalm 133:1

Baa, Baa, Nanny Goat

Baa, Baa, Black Sheep

Baa, baa, nanny goat,
Have you any cheese?
Yes sir, yes sir,
If you please.

Buzz, buzz, busy bee,
Have you any honey?
Yes sir, yes sir,
Do you have money?

Moo, moo, spotted cow,
Have you any cream?
Yes sir, yes sir,
Plenty it seems.

Cluck, cluck, red hen,
Have you any eggs?
Yes sir, yes sir,
Under my legs.

A good man takes care of his animals. Proverbs 12:10 ICB

Merry Are the Bells

Merry Are the Bells

Merry are the bells, and merry would they ring,
Merry are we, and merry will we sing;
With a merry ding-dong, saved, healed, and free,
And a merry sing-song, happy to praise thee!

Merry are the trumpets, and merry would they blare,
Merry are we, and merry will we sing;
With a merry blare-blare, saved, healed, and free,
And a merry blare-blare, happy to praise thee!

Merry are the harps, and merry would they tinkle,
Merry are we, and merry will we sing;
With a merry tinkle-tinkle, saved, healed, and free,
And a merry tinkle-tinkle, happy to praise thee!

Merry are the timbrel, and merry would they jingle,
Merry am I, and merry will I be;
With a merry jingle-jingle, saved, healed, and free,
And a merry jingle-jingle, happy to praise thee!

Merry are the cymbals, and merry would they crash,
Merry are we, and merry will we sing;
With a merry crash-crash, saved, healed, and free,
And a merry crash-crash, happy to praise Thee!

*Praise him with the sounding of the trumpet,
praise him with the harp and lyre,
praise him with tambourine and dancing,
praise him with the strings and flute,
praise him with the clash of cymbals,
praise him with resounding cymbals.
Let everything that has
breath praise the LORD.*
Psalm 150:3-6

Praise the Lord with musical instruments!

Bell	Tap the edges of partially-filled water glasses with a metal spoon. Vary the water levels for different notes.
Trumpet	Roll an 11" x 17" sheet of paper into a tight cone and secure with tape. Blow into the small end.
Harp	Stretch different thicknesses of rubber bands around an empty tissue box. Strum with fingers.
Timbrel	Punch holes at the edge of an aluminum pie tin. Use ribbon to attach jingle bells, paper clips, or any other small metal objects to the ribbons. Shake the timbrel.
Cymbal	Strike the bottom of an empty five-pound coffee can with a spoon.

A merry heart does good, like medicine. . . . **Proverbs 17:22** NKJV

Where Do You Go?

Butterfly, Butterfly, Whence Do You Come?

Butterfly, butterfly, what can you tell?
The Father in heaven does all things well.
Butterfly, butterfly, where do you go?
Where the sun shines, and where the buds grow.

Green frog, green frog, what can you tell?
The Father in heaven does all things well.
Green frog, green frog, where do you go?
Where the pond is cool, and where the brooks flow.

Little bee, little bee, what can you tell?
The Father in heaven does all things well.
Little bee, little bee, where do you go?
Where flowers bloom, and where the breezes blow.

Rabbit, rabbit, what can you tell?
The Father in heaven does all things well.
Rabbit, rabbit, where do you go?
Where there is clover, and where carrots grow.

Black crow, black crow, what can you tell?
The Father in heaven does all things well.
Black crow, black crow, where do you go?
Where there is corn, and where the farmers hoe.

Firefly, firefly, what can you tell?
The Father in heaven does all things well.
Firefly, firefly, where do you go?
Where the moon rises, and where the heavens glow.

But ask the animals what God does.
They will teach you. Or ask the birds of the air.
They will tell you.... Are there any of those
creatures that don't know what the powerful
hand of the LORD has done?
Job 12:7-9 NIrV

Balaam Had a Donkey That Wouldn't Go

If I Had a Donkey That Wouldn't Go

Balaam had a donkey; it went into a ditch.
Did he wallop him? With a switch!

Balaam had a donkey; it ran into a wall.
Did he wallop him? That's not all.

Balaam had a donkey; it wouldn't go.
Did he wallop him? Three times so.

Balaam had a donkey; it spoke to him.
Did he wallop him? Not again!

Balaam had a donkey; it set him straight.
Did he wallop him? No, he prayed.

Read the story of Balaam and his donkey in Numbers 22:21-41.

Jesus Christ Did Pick a Pack of Apt Apostles

Peter Piper Picked a Peck of Pickled Peppers

Jesus Christ did pick a pack of apt apostles,
A pack of apt apostles Jesus Christ did pick.
If Jesus Christ did pick a pack of apt apostles,
Who were the apt apostles Jesus Christ did pick?

James, James, John, and Judas,
Thaddeus and Thomas,
Bartholomew, Simon, Matthew,
And Peter, Philip, Andrew.

Read about Jesus calling the first four disciples in Matthew 4:18-22.

Joshua, Joshua

Humpty Dumpty

Joshua, Joshua marched 'round the wall,
Joshua, Joshua prayed it would fall.
All of his forces,
And all of his men,
Marched around Jericho again and again.

Joshua, Joshua used no force at all.
Joshua, Joshua just marched 'round the wall.
And all of its forces,
And all of its men,
Sat on the wall and laughed at Joshua then.

Joshua, Joshua, shouted and called,
Joshua, Joshua, trumpeted 'round the wall.
All of his forces,
And all of his soldiers,
Rejoiced as the wall crumbled into boulders.

Joshua, Joshua watched Jericho fall,
Joshua, Joshua conquered Jericho's wall.
All of its horses,
And all of its men,
Couldn't keep Joshua's army from rushing in.

Read the story of Joshua and Jericho in Joshua 6.

 CD-2038 *The Gracious Mother Goose*

Solomon Was a Wise Old King

Old King Cole

Faithful Abel was a shepherd man,
And a shepherd man was he.
He gave to the Lord
The best of his flock
And God said, "Your best pleases me."

Trusting Noah was a true believer,
And a true believer was he.
And he listened to God,
And he built an ark,
And he lived through a flood at sea.

Abraham was a very old man,
And a very old man was he.
When he was a hundred,
And Sarah was ninety,
They grew to a family of three.

Joseph was a favorite son,
And a favorite son was he.
He dreamed that the sun,
And the moon and eleven stars
All bowed to him on their knees.

Moses was obedient to God,
And obedient to God was he.
And he told Pharaoh,
"Let my people go,"
And led them through the Red Sea.

Samson was a very strong man,
And a very strong man was he.
And they cut his hair,
And they blinded him,
And he died with his enemies.

Shepherd David, was a very brave boy,
And a very brave boy was he.
With a sling and five stones,
He said to Goliath,
"My God will deliver me."

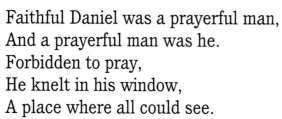

Joshua was a righteous man,
And a righteous man all around.
And he led his army,
'Round Jericho's walls,
And the walls came tumbling down,

Faithful Daniel was a prayerful man,
And a prayerful man was he.
Forbidden to pray,
He knelt in his window,
A place where all could see.

These were all commended for their faith, yet none of them received what had been promised.
God had planned something better for us so that only together with us would they be made perfect.
Hebrews 11:39-40

Puppet Patterns

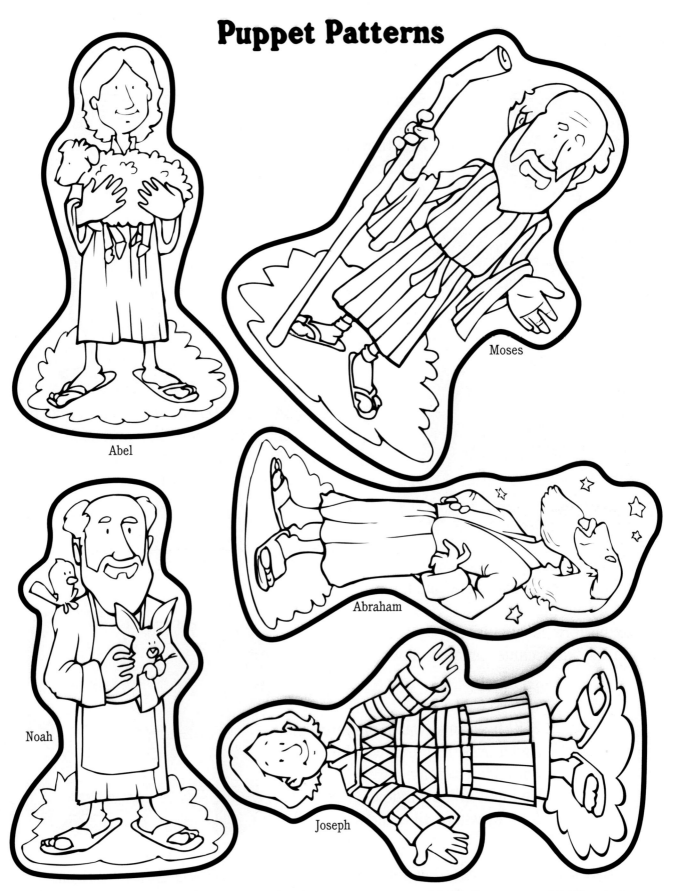

Abel

Moses

Abraham

Noah

Joseph

Use these puppet patterns for extra fun with the poems on pages 26-27. Copy pages 28-29 onto heavy paper. Then, color and cut out the puppets. Attach a craft-stick handle to the back of each.

Puppet Patterns

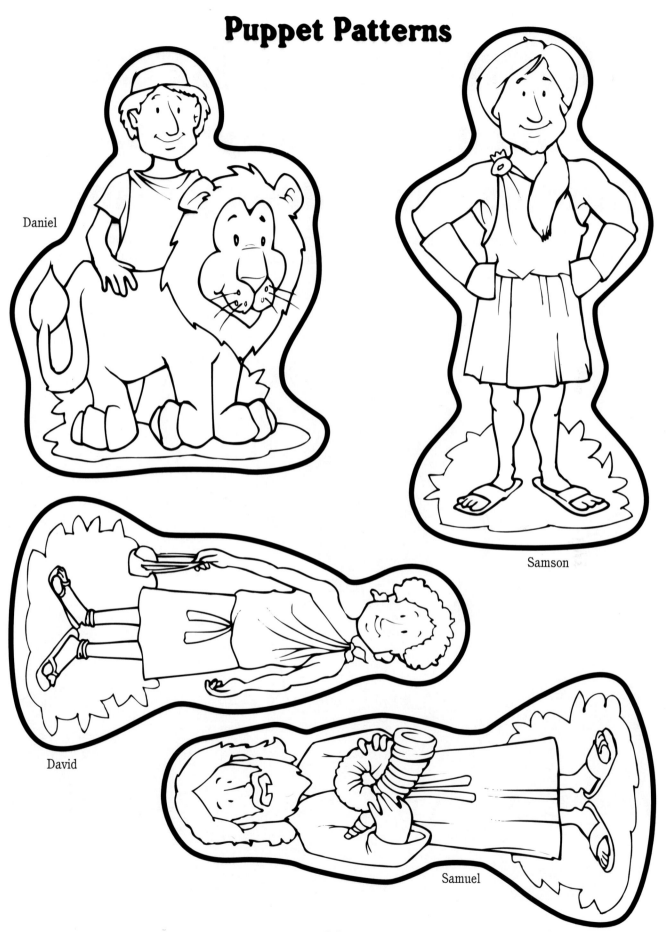

Daniel

Samson

David

Samuel

Chapter Three
Jump Rope Rhymes, Riddles, and Nursery Games

Jump rope or use rhythmic hand movements with these jump rope rhymes.
Use the Scripture references to learn more about the Bible stories or for help with the riddles.

1, 2, 3, 4, 5

Jump once on each number. Jump four times on lines two and four.

1, 2, 3, 4, 5!
Five loaves—two fishes.
6, 7, 8, 9, 10!
Jesus multiplied them.

One for the Father

Jump two times on each line.

One for the Father,
Two for the Son,
Next comes the Spirit,
All three are one.

Ladybug, Ladybug

Jump twice on each line.

Ladybug, ladybug,
Fly away home.
Let your children know
That they are not alone.

Ladybug, ladybug,
How can you know
That the Lord is with you
And you're never alone?

Ladybug, ladybug,
God told us so.
The truth is in the Bible
And that's how we know!

Little Jumping Joan

Jump four times on each line.

Here am I, little jumping Joan,
When nobody's with me, I'm not alone.
Here am I, little jumping Joan,
Since Jesus is with me, I'm never alone.

One To Make Ready

Jump twice on each line.

One to make ready,
And two to prepare,
God bless the rider,
And away goes the mare.

One, Two

Jump four times on each line.

One, two, Jesus loves you.
Three, four, He's at the door.
Five, six, you He picks,
Seven, eight, please don't wait.
Nine, ten, invite Him in!

Jack Be Nimble

While chanting the rhyme, two children turn the rope and
substitute a child's name for Jack. The child jumps in
and recites a Bible verse while jumping.

Jack be nimble,
Jack be quick.
Jump right in
And say your pick.

Read how the name of Jesus caused a crippled man to jump in Acts 3:1-10.

Great A, Little a

Jump two times on each line.

Great A, little a,
Beautiful B!
Christ gives me courage,
And He strengthens me.

Great D, little d,
Excellent E!
Our Father lives forever,
And so will we.

Great G, little g,
Heavenly H!
I am so imperfect,
I'll get better with age.

Great J, little j,
Kindly K!
The Lord will never leave us.
He is with us always.

Great M, little m,
Noble N!
Open hearts will offer Him,
A welcomed place within.

Great P, little p,
Quiet Q!
Rejoice in our Redeemer,
And He'll live with you.

Great S, little s,
Thoughtful T!
Unequaled in the universe,
He loves me.

Great V, little v,
Willing W!
eXcellent is the Word
To hear and to do.

Great Y, little y,
Zealous Z!
Verses start to finish,
All in praise of Thee.

"I am the Alpha and the Omega," says the Lord God,
"who is, and who was, and who is to come, the Almighty."
Revelation 1:8

Punch and Judy

Jump four times on each line until you miss a jump.

Punch and Judy fought for a pie.
Punch gave Judy a knock in the eye.
Says Judy to Punch, "Hitting is a sin."
Says Punch to Judy, "Forgive me, my friend."

Says Judy to Punch, "All right, I do."
Says Punch to Judy, "That's good of you."
Says Judy to Punch, "To be forgiven . . ."
Says Punch to Judy, ". . . forgive seventy times seven."

How many times, would that be?
Seventy times seven is four hundred ninety
One, two, three, four, five, ...

*Jesus said to him, "I do not say to you,
up to seven times, but up to seventy times seven.*
Matthew 18:22 NKJV

Hark, Hark

Jump four times on each line; then jump
and count as fast as possible.

Hark, hark, the dogs do bark,
The liars are all around;
On TV screens and magazines,
And some from Hollywood town.

*Who is a liar but he who
denies that Jesus is the Christ?*
1 John 2:22 NKJV

Riddles

Women of the Bible
Little Maid, Little Maid, Whither Goest Thou?

Big sister, big sister,
Whither goest thou?
To float baby brother,
Where he will be found.

Wise woman, wise woman,
Whither goest thou?
To judge my people,
Beneath the shady bough.

Daughter-in-law, daughter-in-law,
Whither goest thou?
To glean the grain,
Before they plow.

Pretty queen, pretty queen,
Whither goest thou?
To beg the king's mercy,
For our people now.

Read about these women in: Exodus 2:4, Judges 4:4-5, Ruth 2:2-3, Esther 7:3.

 CD-2038 *The Gracious Mother Goose*

Tell Me What You Think

Mary at the Cottage Door

One, two, three, four,
Samson at Delilah's door;
Five, six, seven, eight,
Did she love? Did she hate?
Tell me what you think.

One, two, three, four,
Samuel at Eli's door;
Five, six, seven, eight,
Did he wake him, did he wait?
Tell me what you think.

One, two, three, four,
Elisha at Elijah's door;
Five, six, seven, eight,
Did he follow? Did he wait?
Tell me what you think.

One, two, three, four,
The Lord at Solomon's door;
Five, six, seven, eight,
Name his wish. What was his fate?
Tell me what you think.

Read about these people in: Judges 16:18-19, 1 Samuel 3:8-9, 2 Kings 2:2, 2 Chronicles 1:11-12.

Mom, Oh Mom, Whose Mom Art Thou?

Bow-Wow-Wow, Whose Dog Art Thou?

Mom, oh Mom,
Whose Mom art thou?
Little Seth was my son.
Can you name me now?

Mom, oh Mom,
Whose Mom art thou?
Little Isaac was my son.
Can you name me now?

Mom, oh Mom,
Whose Mom art thou?
Jacob and Esau were my sons,
Can you name me now?

Mom, oh Mom,
Whose Mom art thou?
Joseph and Benjamin were my sons,
Can you name me now?

Mom, oh Mom,
Whose Mom art thou?
Little Samuel was my son,
Can you name me now?

Mom, oh Mom,
Whose Mom art thou?
Little Obed was my son,
Can you name me now?

Mom, oh Mom,
Whose Mom art thou?
John the Baptist was my son.
Can you name me now?

Mom, oh Mom,
Whose Mom art thou?
Jesus was my special son,
Can you name me now?

Read about these famous moms in:
Genesis 4:25, Genesis 17:19, Genesis 25:24-26, Genesis 29:9 and 35:24,
1 Samuel 1:20, Ruth 4:13-17, Luke 1:13, Matthew 1:18.

 CD-2038 *The Gracious Mother Goose*

Nursery Games

Brow Brinky

Point to facial feature on each line.

> Brow brinky,
> Eye winky,
> Cheek cherry,
> Mouth merry,
> Nose noppy,
> Chin choppy.

Eye Winker

Point to facial feature on each line.

> Head thinker,
> Eye winker,
> Nose smeller,
> Mouth eater,
> Chin chopper.

Here Is the Church

Lace fingers, point index fingers up to make steeple, turn palms up, wiggle fingers.

> Here is the church.
> Here is the steeple.
> Open the door
> And see all the people.

Ride a Cock–Horse

Bounce child on foot while holding hands.

> Ride a cock-horse to Sunday School,
> Just like a fine lady/gent, upon a white horse;
> Hold tight with your fingers; hold tight with your toes,
> He shall ride safely wherever He goes.

I praise you because I am fearfully and wonderfully made;
your works are wonderful, I know that full well.
Psalm 139:14

Chapter Four
Song and Dance

Sing and make music in your heart to the Lord with these songs and movement games!

Here We Go 'Round God's Green Earth

Here We Go 'Round the Mulberry Bush

Hold hands and walk in a circle while singing the chorus.

When singing the verses, drop hands and move in appropriate ways.

Chorus

Here we go 'round God's green Earth,
God's green Earth, God's green Earth,
Here we go 'round God's green Earth,
Early in the morning.

Verse 1

Stiff-kneed, move back and forth on feet.

This is the way we waddle like ducks,
Waddle like ducks, waddle like ducks,
This is the way we waddle like ducks,
Early in the morning.

Verse 2

Lift knees high and gallop about.

This is the way we prance like ponies,
Prance like ponies, prance like ponies,
This is the way we prance like ponies,
Early in the morning.

Additional Verses

This is the way we lope like llamas.

Use a long, easy stride.

This is the way we trot like tigers.

Use a jogging gait—between a walk and run.

This is the way we strut like peacocks.

Walk in a proud way.

This is the way we amble like elephants.

Use a slow, leisurely walk. Touch shoulder to nose, and swing arm like a trunk.

This is the way we sway like camels.

Walk moving back and forth from side to side.

This is the way we gallop like gazelles.

Run, bringing both feet off the ground at times.

This is the way we hop like frogs.

Jump forward with feet together.

This is the way we laze like lizards.

Lie still on belly.

This is the way we slither like snakes.

On belly, move along with a sliding or gliding motion.

This is the way we creep like turtles.

On all fours, move along very slowly.

This is the way we swoop like swallows.

Slowly flap arms at the same time, like a bird soaring.

This is the way we swim like seals.

Hands at sides, move in a slow, smooth way as if gliding in water.

This is the way we skulk like skunks.

Move as if trying to hide.

This is the way we crawl like snails.

On belly, arms down to the side, propel forward inch by inch.

This is the way we pose like possums.

Freeze and stay still.

This is the way we leap like leopards.

Squat with hands on ground between legs and jump forward.

I own every bird in the mountains. The creatures of the field belong to me. Psalm 50:11 NIrV

Sing a Song, Sing a Song, Little Man

Pat-a-Cake, Pat-a-Cake, Baker's Man

Sing a song, sing a song, little man.
Sing me a song as fast as you can.
Sing high, and sing low, and always sing on key.
And there will be music for you and me.

Say a prayer, say a prayer, little man.
Say a prayer as fast as you can.
Pray for you, pray for me, and pray for all our kin.
God will surely bless us all. Amen and amen!

When a good man prays,
great things happen.
James 5:16 ICB

Rock–a–Bye, Baby

Hush-a-Bye, Baby

Rock-a-bye, baby, in the tree top,
When the wind blows, the cradle will rock.
When the bough bends, the cradle will sway,
And you will sleep safely all through the day.

He has put his angels in charge of you. They will watch over you wherever you go. Psalm 91:11 ICB

The Shepherd Had One Hundred Sheep

Mary Had a Little Lamb

The shepherd had one hundred sheep
With fleece as white as snow,
And everywhere the shepherd went
His flock was sure to go.

Until one day one careless ewe,
While grazing went astray.
It made the shepherd worry so
To lose a lamb that way.

The shepherd went to search it out,
And found its trail nearby.
It wandered thoughtlessly about,
Till it saw its master's eye.

Why did He leave the ninety-nine
In search of just one ewe?
Because he greatly loves his lambs
Like Jesus Christ loves you.

In the same way your Father in heaven is not willing that any of these little ones should be lost.
Matthew 18:14

Faithful Noah Built an Ark

Old MacDonald Had a Farm

Faithful Noah built an ark. E-I-E-I-O
And on the ark there were two pigs. E-I-E-I-O
With an oink-oink here and an oink-oink there,
Here an oink, there an oink,
Everywhere an oink-oink.
Faithful Noah built an ark. E-I-E-I-O

Faithful Noah built an ark. E-I-E-I-O
And on the ark there were two cats. E-I-E-I-O
With a meow-meow here and a meow-meow there,
Here a meow, there a meow,
Everywhere a meow-meow.
Faithful Noah built an ark. E-I-E-I-O

Read about animals on the ark in Genesis 7:1-5.

More animals and sounds:

dogs	bow-wow	geese	honk-honk
chicks	peep-peep	chickens	cluck-cluck
cows	moo-moo	frogs	ribbit-ribbit
lambs	baa-baa	lions	roar-roar
ducks	quack-quack	bears	grrr-grrr
horses	neigh-neigh	birds	chirp-chirp
donkeys	eha-eha	mice	squeak-squeak
crows	caw-caw	coyotes	yip-yip
bees	buzz-buzz	lizards	hiss-hiss

Oh, Do You Know the Son of God?

Do You Know the Muffin Man?

Oh, do you know the Son of God,
The Son of God, the Son of God,
Oh, do you know the Son of God,
Born on Christmas Day?

Oh, do you know Jesus Christ,
Jesus Christ, Jesus Christ,
Oh, do you know Jesus Christ,
Who came to show the way?

Oh, do you know the perfect man,
The perfect man, the perfect man,
Oh, do you know the perfect man,
Who taught us how to pray?

Oh, do you know the Lamb of God,
The Lamb of God? The Lamb of God,
Oh, do you know the Lamb of God,
Who rose on Easter morn?

We know that we have come to know him if we obey his commands. 1 John 2:3

Jericho's Wall

London Bridge Is Falling Down

Jericho's wall is coming down,
Coming down, coming down.
Jericho's wall is coming down,
I hear marching!

Jericho's wall is coming down,
Coming down, coming down.
Jericho's wall is coming down,
I hear trumpets!

Jericho's wall is coming down,
Coming down, coming down.
Jericho's wall is coming down,
I hear shouting!

As soon as the fighting men heard the [trumpets],
they gave a loud shout. Then the wall fell down. Joshua 6:20 NIrV

It Didn't Stop Them

If You're Happy and You Know It

Scorn and laughter didn't stop Noah's ark.
Scorn and laughter didn't stop Noah's ark.
He built it on dry ground,
The laughter soon was drowned.
Scorn and laughter didn't stop Noah's ark.

Old age did not stop Abraham.
Old age did not stop Abraham.
He proved that he had patience,
And he fathered many nations.
Old age did not stop Abraham.

Jealous brothers didn't stop Joseph's dreams.
Jealous brothers didn't stop Joseph's dreams.
They sold him as a slave,
But his dreams would Egypt save.
Jealous brothers didn't stop Joseph's dreams.

Being small didn't stop David's aim.
Being small didn't stop David's aim.
With a sling and a stone,
He killed a giant on his own.
Being small didn't stop David's aim.

A den of lions didn't stop Daniel's faith.
A den of lions didn't stop Daniel's faith.
He worshipped, knelt, and prayed,
In his window, unafraid.
A den of lions didn't stop Daniel's faith.

A fiery furnace didn't stop Abednego.
A fiery furnace didn't stop Abednego.
With him, Shadrach took his turn,
Even Meshach didn't burn.
A fiery furnace didn't stop Abednego.

. . . people who don't give up are blessed. James 5:11 NIrV

Jesus Is His Name

Bingo

Clap each time a letter is omitted.

I have a Friend I love so much.
Jesus is His name. Yes!
J-E-S-U-S
J-E-S-U-S
J-E-S-U-S
And Jesus is His name. Yes!

I have a Friend I love so much.
Jesus is His name. Yes!
(clap once) E-S-U-S
(clap once) E-S-U-S
(clap once) E-S-U-S
And Jesus is His name. Yes!

I have a Friend I love so much.
Jesus is His name. Yes!
(clap twice) S-U-S
(clap twice) S-U-S
(clap twice) S-U-S
And Jesus is His name. Yes!

I have a Friend I love so much.
Jesus is His name. Yes!
(clap 3 times) U-S
(clap 3 times) U-S
(clap 3 times) U-S
And Jesus is His name. Yes!

I have a Friend I love so much.
Jesus is His name. Yes!
(clap 4 times) S
(clap 4 times) S
(clap 4 times) S
And Jesus is His name. Yes!

I have a Friend I love so much.
Jesus is His name. Yes!
(clap 5 times)
(clap 5 times)
(clap 5 times)
And Jesus is His name. Yes!

Therefore God exalted him to the highest place and gave him the name that is above every name, that at the name of Jesus every knee should bow. . . .
Philippians 2:9-10

We Will See Him in the Clouds when He Comes

She'll Be Coming 'Round the Mountain

We will see Him in the clouds when He comes.
We will see Him in the clouds when He comes.
We will see Him in the clouds,
We will see Him in the clouds,
We will see Him in the clouds when He comes.

Angel choirs will sing Hosanna when He comes.
Angel choirs will sing Hosanna when He comes.
Angel choirs will sing Hosanna,
Angel choirs will sing Hosanna,
Angel choirs will sing Hosanna when He comes.

There'll be shouts of Hallelujah when He comes.
There'll be shouts of Hallelujah when He comes.
There'll be shouts of Hallelujah,
There'll be shouts of Hallelujah,
There'll be shouts of Hallelujah when He comes.

He will take us up to heaven when He comes.
He will take us up to heaven when He comes.
He will take us up to heaven,
He will take us up to heaven,
He will take us up to heaven when He comes.

Look! He is coming with the clouds! Every eye will see him. Revelation 1:7 NIrV

Chapter Five
Bible Stories in Rhyme

These original rhymes will familiarize children with the greatest stories ever told!

In the Beginning

Day one, God said,
"Let there be light."
The light He called day;
The dark He called night.

Day two, God divided
Heaven from Earth.
To a brand-new world
Our Lord God gave birth.

Day three, God divided
Dry land and seas.
He brought forth the grass,
Its seeds and fruit trees.

Day four, God created
The Heavenly lights.
Sun, Moon, and stars
Ruled the days and the nights.

Day five, God spoke life
In the seas and the skies,
Minnows, great whales,
Condors, magpies.

Day six, God made
The beasts of the land.
And in His own image
Woman and man.

Day seven, God rested
From His mighty feat.
He saw it was good.
His work was complete.

Read about the first seven days in Genesis 1 and 2:1-2.

 CD-2038 *The Gracious Mother Goose*

Noah's Story

One fair morn God spoke to me,
"Build an ark, Noah, carefully."
The neighbors laughed.
I finished the task.
I prayed to know what was to be.

All the beasts came by twos:
Butterflies, turtles, bears, emus,
Giraffes and rhinos,
Flamingos and hippos,
Loons, baboons, and kangaroos.

God shut us in the rain-proof ark,
As the heavens turned extremely dark.
The rain splashed,
The thunder crashed.
The lightning flashed in jagged sparks.

For forty days the rain did fall,
And mighty waters covered all.
In God's safe hand,
My dove found land,
Returning with a branch so small.

When on dry land, God promised me,
"Look above and you shall see,
A rainbow sky,
Which says that I
Will not again o'rflow the sea."

Read about Noah in Genesis 6-9.

Moses' Story

In a bulrush basket,
Floating on the water,
Little baby Moses
Was found by Pharaoh's daughter.

He grew up in the palace,
Prince of all the land.
Until he killed a savage guard
And fled into the sand.

Upon a mountain God did speak.
From a bush aflame,
"Go to see the Pharaoh,
Your people's freedom claim."

"Mighty Pharaoh," Moses said,
"Let my people go."
As a warning, God sent plagues,
But Egypt's king said, "No!"

Moses lofted his good staff
And ripped apart the sea.
Pharaoh's army all was drowned,
And Israel was set free.

Waiting at the mountain's foot,
The people danced and laughed.
While God carved His Law in stone,
They built a golden calf.

For forty years they wandered,
Through a wilderness of sand,
Till at last it came to pass,
They reached the promised land.

Read about Moses and the children of Israel in the book of Exodus.

Mary's Story

Long ago and far away, a heavenly angel came
To a maid so young and fair; he called her by her name.
"Mary, God has chosen you as mother of His Son."
Said the angel, "Name Him Jesus. He's the Blessed One."

Mary didn't understand all that she had heard.
Unafraid, she knelt and prayed about the angel's words.
An angel spoke to Joseph then, "Take her for your wife."
He obeyed and married her to cherish all his life.

Weary Mary swayed for days, a plodding donkey's load.
As Joseph led to Bethlehem along the dusty road.
When they arrived, all inns were full, which left them quite forlorn.
They could not sleep upon the street, the child would soon be born.

Then at last a kind man said, "In my stable, stay."
And on that night the babe was placed in a manger full of hay.
A new star rose and Mary sang her sweetest lullaby,
To her baby, son of God, beneath the Christmas sky.

The beasts then welcomed Baby Jesus with a heartfelt song.
Cows mooed; doves cooed; donkeys brayed together all night long.
On hillsides, shepherds watched their flocks upon that holy night.
They heard a voice, "Be not afraid," while the Lord's glory shone bright.

The angel told them, "Christ is born in Bethlehem this day."
Then the shepherds left their sheep and found Him on the hay.
Wise men three, on camels tall, took gifts of spice and gold.
They traveled far toward the star through miles of wind and cold.

They asked King Herod where to find this Holy newborn King.
"When you find this child, return and his location bring."
They found the child beneath the star, so innocent and fair,
They worshipped there and laid before Him treasures dear and rare.

To the wise men in a dream an angel spoke a warning.
Herod is a wicked king, don't see him in the morning.
Joseph dreamed of danger, too. The angel said, "Don't stay!
The king desires to kill the babe; to Egypt run away!"

Joseph heeding all he heard, with Mary and her Son,
Traveled to another land and saved the Blessed One.
This Christmas story doesn't end with the tale of Jesus' birth.
The Holy Child was born to be the Savior of the Earth!

Read about Mary in Luke 1:26; 2

Jesus' Story

At a simple wedding feast
He turned water into wine.
Of this wonder Jesus said,
"'Tis God's work, the glory Thine."

Jesus healed the mother
Of Peter's grieving wife.
A faithful ruler's daughter,
He soon brought back to life.

The sightless saw, the crippled walked,
The sick were all made whole.
Through faith, He healed their bodies.
With love, He healed their souls.

Five thousand hungry people
Miraculously were fed,
With just two little fishes
And five small loaves of bread.

The winds and waves obeyed Him.
He calmed the storm-tossed sea.
Jesus walked on water,
And beckoned, "Come to me."

Four days the corpse of Lazarus
Inside the tomb lay cold.
Jesus saved His friend from death,
Brought others to the fold.

Miracle of miracles!
He conquered cross and grave.
Jesus rose on Easter morn,
A dying world to save.

Jesus Christ is the same yesterday and today and forever. Hebrews 13:8

The Easter Story

To Jerusalem, Jesus came;
People shouted, "Praise His name."

Temple money changers fled;
When "Leave my Father's house!" He said.

He taught the truth to those who came.
With love He healed the blind and lame.

Traitor Judas sold his Brother;
Jesus said, "Love one another."

He gave disciples bread and wine;
Then He prayed, "God's will, not mine."

Friday He was crucified;
As it was written, Jesus died.

The disciples ran away in fear;
The women wept most bitter tears.

Easter morn, he left the grave;
Joy and wonder, Jesus saves!

Read about the Easter story in Matthew 21-28.

Chapter Six
Holiday Performances

The performing arts can be a fun and meaningful way to bring glory to the Lord!
The following rhymes are especially suited for staging, but any rhyme, riddle, or story in this book
can be used in a skit or musical performance. See pages 63-64 for staging and costume ideas.

A Christmas Song

To perform as a musical skit, have players appear on stage at appropriate times.

On the First Christmas Morning

On the First Day of Christmas

On the first Christmas morning,
The Lord gave to us
A tiny, baby Jesus.

On the first Christmas morning,
The Lord gave to us
Two parents praying,
And a tiny, baby Jesus.

On the first Christmas morning,
The Lord gave to us
Three wise men seeking,
Two parents praying,
And a tiny, baby Jesus.

On the first Christmas morning,
The Lord gave to us
Four shepherds kneeling
Three wise men seeking
Two parents praying.
And a tiny, baby Jesus.

On the first Christmas morning,
The Lord gave to us
Five angels singing,
Four shepherds kneeling,
Three wise men seeking,
Two parents praying,
And a tiny, baby Jesus.

On the first Christmas morning,
The Lord gave to us
Six cows mooing,
Five angels singing,
Four shepherds kneeling,
Three wise men seeking,
Two parents praying,
And a tiny, baby Jesus.

On the first Christmas morning,
The Lord gave to us
Seven doves cooing,
Six cows mooing,
Five angels singing,
Four shepherds kneeling,
Three wise men seeking,
Two parents praying,
And a tiny, baby Jesus.

On the first Christmas morning,
The Lord gave to us
Eight hens laying,
Seven doves cooing,
Six cows mooing,
Five angels singing,
Four shepherds kneeling,
Three wise men seeking,
Two parents praying,
And a tiny, baby Jesus.

On the first Christmas morning,
The Lord gave to us
Nine donkeys braying,
Eight hens laying,
Seven doves cooing,
Six cows mooing,
Five angels singing,
Four shepherds kneeling,
Three wise men seeking,
Two parents praying,
And a tiny, baby Jesus.

On the first Christmas morning,
The Lord gave to us
Ten horses neighing,
Nine donkeys braying,
Eight hens laying,
Seven doves cooing,
Six cows mooing,
Five angels singing,
Four shepherds kneeling,
Three wise men seeking,
Two parents praying,
And a tiny, baby Jesus.

On the first Christmas morning,
The Lord gave to us
Eleven soldiers riding,
Ten horses neighing,
Nine donkeys braying,
Eight hens laying,
Seven doves cooing,
Six cows mooing,
Five angels singing.
Four shepherds kneeling,
Three wise men seeking,
Two parents praying,
And a tiny, baby Jesus.

On the first Christmas morning,
The Lord gave to us
Twelve stars shining,
Eleven soldiers riding,
Ten horses neighing,
Nine donkeys braying,
Eight hens laying,
Seven doves cooing,
Six cows mooing,
Five angels singing,
Four shepherds kneeling,
Three wise men seeking,
Two parents praying,
And a tiny, baby Jesus.

...she gave birth to her first-born, a son. She wrapped him in cloths and placed him in a manger, because there was no room for them in the inn.
Luke 2:7

A Christmas Play

To perform as a play, have players appear on stage at appropriate times.

Road to Bethlehem
This Is the House That Jack Built

This is the road to Bethlehem.

These are the camels that plodded and swayed
Along the road to Bethlehem.

Here are three wise men with precious gifts
Who came on camels that plodded and swayed
Along the road to Bethlehem.

Here are the angels that sweetly sang
While three wise men with precious gifts
Came on camels that plodded and swayed
Along the road to Bethlehem.

These are the shepherds, watching their flocks,
Who heard the angels that sweetly sang
While three wise men with precious gifts
Came on camels that plodded and swayed
Along the road to Bethlehem.

This is the star that brightened the sky
Above the shepherds, watching their flocks,
Who heard the angels that sweetly sang
While three wise men with precious gifts
Came on camels that plodded and swayed
Along the road to Bethlehem.

This is the inn, crowded and loud,
Under the star that brightened the sky
Above the shepherds, watching their flocks,
Who heard the angels that sweetly sang
While three wise men with precious gifts
Came on camels that plodded and swayed
Along the road to Bethlehem.

This is the stable, humble and low,
Behind the inn, crowded and loud,
Under the star that brightened the sky
Above the shepherds, watching their flocks,
Who heard the angels that sweetly sang
While three wise men with precious gifts
Came on camels that plodded and swayed
Along the road to Bethlehem.

Here are the animals, great beasts and small,
That shared the stable, humble and low,
Behind the inn, crowded and loud,
Under the star that brightened the sky
Above the shepherds, watching their flocks,
Who heard the angels that sweetly sang
While three wise men with precious gifts
Came on camels that plodded and swayed
Along the road to Bethlehem.

This man is Joseph, loving and kind,
Who calmed the animals, great beasts and small,
That shared the stable, humble and low,
Behind the inn, crowded and loud,
Under the star that brightened the sky
Above the shepherds, watching their flocks,
Who heard the angels that sweetly sang
While three wise men with precious gifts
Came on camels that plodded and swayed
Along the road to Bethlehem.

Here's gentle Mary, favored by God
And cherished by Joseph, loving and kind,
Who calmed the animals, great beasts and small,
That shared the stable, humble and low,
Behind the inn, crowded and loud,
Under the star that brightened the sky
Above the shepherds, watching their flocks,
Who heard the angels that sweetly sang
While three wise men with precious gifts
Came on camels that plodded and swayed
Along the road to Bethlehem.

This is the babe, laid in a manger
By gentle Mary, favored by God
And cherished by Joseph, loving and kind,
Who calmed the animals, great beasts and small,
That shared the stable, humble and low,
Behind the inn, crowded and loud,
Under the star that brightened the sky
Above the shepherds, watching their flocks,
Who heard the angels that sweetly sang
While three wise men with precious gifts
Came on camels that plodded and swayed
Along the road to Bethlehem.

Read the Christmas story in Luke 2.

An Easter Song

Sing to the tune of *Twinkle, Twinkle Little Star*. Have a child quietly stand in a spotlight with a stuffed donkey or other representation. During each verse, an appropriate prop is placed near the donkey. (Props: basket of bread and fish, crown of thorns, cross, a child wearing a robe with nail prints in his hands) Begin and end the presentation with a trumpet solo.

Donkey, Donkey, Old and Gray

Donkey, Donkey, Old and Gray

(trumpet solo to the tune *Twinkle, Twinkle Little Star*)

Donkey, donkey, old and gray,
Open your mouth and gently bray.
Lift your ears and blow your horn,
To praise the miracles He performs.
Donkey, donkey, old and gray,
Open your mouth and gently bray.

Donkey, donkey, old and gray,
Open your mouth and gently bray.
Lift your ears and blow your horn,
To tell about His crown of thorns.
Donkey, donkey, old and gray,
Open your mouth and gently bray.

Donkey, donkey, old and gray,
Open your mouth and gently bray.
Lift your ears and blow your horn,
To cheer a grieving world forlorn.
Donkey, donkey, old and gray,
Open your mouth and gently bray.

Donkey, donkey, old and gray,
Open your mouth and gently bray.
Lift your ears and blow your horn,
To tell He rose on Easter morn.
Donkey, donkey, old and gray,
Open your mouth and gently bray.

(repeat trumpet solo)

*"Do not be afraid, O Daughter of Zion;
see, your king is coming,
seated on a donkey's colt."*
John 12:15

Presentation Ideas

Pantomimes

Pantomimes may be one of the easiest ways to present rhymes and stories. After hearing the story, players just act out the story without saying lines. *Balaam Had a Donkey* (page 22) works well as a pantomime.

Individual Readings

Have each child choose his favorite rhyme to read or memorize and present. On performance day, have children take turns giving their individual selections for a great variety show!

Shadow Shows

Place a light behind a large white sheet stretched taut and suspended from a clothesline or rope. Darken the room as much as possible. While someone reads a selection, the actors move back and forth between the sheet and the light. During breaks in the story or scenes, the light is turned off while the reader announces the next scene or story.

Radio Dramas

This creative and fun method requires no memorization. Create scripts and record children on a cassette tape recorder. Encourage children to think of appropriate sound effects.

Puppet Plays

Create a puppet stage and allow children to either memorize or read their lines. Use the puppet patterns on pages 28-29.

Choral Readings

One Line per Child

Practice to make the timing seamless from one person to the next.

Solo and Chorus

Various children recite certain lines and then the group joins together for the chorus. This type of reading works well for small children.

Choir and Chorus

Group children into Choir 1 and Choir 2. Each choir speaks its assigned parts in unison. Then, both choirs speak the chorus.

Unison Speaking

The group speaks as one person. This requires practice for perfect timing, balance, phrasing, and harmony in inflection.

Videos

Video taping allows children the opportunity to start over and correct mistakes. Video tape children performing one or more rhymes. Edit and add music or graphics as desired. Allow children to start over, correct mistakes, and record again.

Tableaus

Tableau means "living picture." In this type of performance, the group stands costumed and posed while a narrator reads the story. Curtains may be opened and closed in between new poses.

Operettas

Choose a theme for the operetta such as Bible characters or poems and prayers, and intersperse musical selections with recitations for performances that everyone will enjoy!

Costumes

Biblical Robes

Use twin-sized flat sheets in solid colors or stripes. Fold a sheet in half and cut as illustrated. Stitch the side and underarm seams. Hem all rough edges by turning up once. Tie with a strip of fabric around the waist.

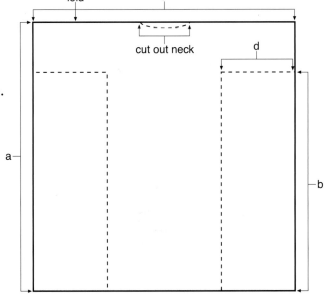

a = Measure shoulder to ankle.

b = Measure underarm to ankle.

c = Measure extended arms, fingertip to fingertip.

d = Measure underarm to extended fingertip.

Kings and Queens

Kings and queens can wear bright colors and several pieces of jewelry. The addition of gold or silver braid to the hem and sleeves will add a royal appearance. Crowns can be made from gold poster board adorned with braid, sequins, or fake gem stones. For headbands, arm bands, or bracelets, cut strips of poster board and staple ends to form a circle. Cover with foil or gold paper and decorate with sequins or glitter.

Shepherds

Head coverings for shepherds can be made with striped or burlap-type material. Cut a 36" x 36" piece of cloth. Place on head and secure with braided strips of fabric so that it hangs down in the back. Shepherds can carry a wooden stick for a staff.

Angels

Angels can wear robes made from used white sheets. Add gold braid or rickrack around the neck and hem. Create a belt with the same gold trim. A headband of Christmas tinsel can serve as a halo.